CONTENTS

RAGGED STAR

Gerry McDonnell

DEDICATED TO MY FATHER

PART I

Ragged Star

I

I must have gurgled
and balled
in the house on leafy heights
bought for cash
one hundred foot garden
greyhounds, pony and trap
Bedford van and *Austin Cambridge*
business thriving
workers stuffing fivers down their bras.
A family photo
with me on his lap
neither very happy.

II

Then a climb down
to a modest, terraced house
under a ragged star
Easter eggs
cooling in the window sill
squeaky wrapped and ribboned
to bring in a few bob.

III

Then further down
crossing the river
to the flood line.
The move at night
horror at the thought
furniture on horse and cart
What'll the neighbours think?
He sat up on the cart.
I walked with her.

IV

The house was old and damp
reclaimed from the sea.
One time haunt of
pirates and highwaymen.
He had a troop of handy men
to keep decay at bay.
Mad Joe for rotting floors
and poisoned rats.
Keltch for mismatched wallpaper.
A gardener watched over
don't forget that bit there.
A painter
for maroon or grained hall door
a shake in his hand.

Nixers settled in the pub.

V

The house
backed onto the river.
I being sickly
slept in the box room
the gulls craving
sunlight buttering lace curtains
convalescing for days
at the top of the stairs
in fear at night
with just the landing light
or worse
crying out
a kerfuffle in the hall
a diagnosis,
the bulb is gone.

VI

In the divvying of beds
six to a small house
him being strong
slept by a weeping wall
with murder magazines
smoked in the dark
each pull
alerting an assassin
to a head shot.

At seven we shared a bed
knees against his cold behind.

At three,
I came between them
even in the marriage bed, he said.

VII

In the confessional
my knees hurt.
I confess to Almighty God...
Orchards robbed
sixpence taken from his jacket pocket
a song bird shot from a branch
bead of blood on red breast heaving.

Fifty years of guilt.
I confessed only the first.

VIII

Sunday, church-spelled air
struck dumb
no one coming out
against street play
only priest-approved GAA.
At ten, the pictures
at THE BLIND.
Hard benches
albino children at the front
squinting at the flickering images.
At twelve, THE FAIRVIEW
From Russia with Love.
Then tea and homework.
Pencil, rubber, steel triangle
palimpsest
attempts puffed away.

Present among night sounds –
doors opening
and closing
radio dying –
the awful swish of Monday.

IX

On Sunday the last gasp Mass
down to kneel
on the granite steps.

Inside blood drained from me in the aisle.
Would the host recoil?
Some mortal sin in the recesses?
I made it back
tongue twisting at the body and blood
stuck to the roof of my mouth.

As the congregation stirred
the men roused themselves
and headed for the lunchtime session.

X

On Sunday he lowered
fizzing Liver Salts
to flush out the week.
Here, take a half spoon.
We waited near the toilet
for the pressure to build.
He went first
window opened
fags and *News of the World*
a pungent smell of hops
lingering.

XI

Well-chested
sputum green
out sick from school
then back again.
The dead arose and appeared to many.
Accustomed to desk smell and grain
but soon gone again.

Muscles like knots on thread.
Legs like two straws
hanging from a loft.
Be careful goin' over the gratin's
but don't worry
your ears'll hold you up.

All said in jest, of course.
Teasing, a practiced black art
born of a paucity of love.

XII

A foreign tongue at home
remnants only
on my mother's side.
Flaithiulach¹.
Not in the hungry fifties.
Corduroy pair for hard wear
short trousers sniffy
zipped jacket.
Lambs to the lashing
and mocking.
Spits brandishing *an leather²*
six of the best on each hand
to break in the new boy, a *Sasanach³*
Fr McShane wanting a feel.
The results
a distain for the 'cloth'
dispossessed.

¹ *Generous*

² *Leather strap to administer corporal punishment in Irish schools.*

³ *Englishman*

XIII

Freed from algebra
studs clacking on the streets
on our way to the naked park
frisky with football flair.
On the pitch
not all we made it out to be
us Icaruses
with muddy boots
and heavy, grounded ball.

XIV

We went to go
at the same time.
Come on
sure we're both the same.
Two streams splashing, frothing.
I couldn't
further frustration.

Mid-stream is medicinal
it seems.

XV

Proof of name and address.
Playing football
on the street, Your Honour.
I knocked the hall door down
but he was out to the world.
I climbed through the window
up to him sleeping
catching a few hours kip.
I shook him
a fearful intimacy
until he turned and looked at me
confused.

XVI

I waited for
the dangling voice of Summer-work.
Come in!
The official scratched for the sense
in English, Philosophy and Psychology.
What kind of job
will you get out of that?
Clipping his toe nails
foot on desk
crescents skimming the lino floor.
How many years have you left?
Do any of us know?
He gave me a look.
His Spring and Summer gone I thought
and most of Autumn too
Winter waving up ahead.
He shaped up
pulled on his sock
and laced his shoe.
Now, did you work with us before?

XVII

He coached me
on the sports day.
Take a raw egg and lie down.
I shot out but fell back
feeling his absence on the sideline.
Just as well!

XVIII

I worried the mirror
thinking my limbs
and lips thin rivulets.
Impatient for
the five o' clock shadow.
He's startin' to smell himself.
You've a lovely mouth
for coolin' soup!
Lady's hands have I?
Stiffened socks.

IXX

From ink well to THE TALBOT PRESS
the secrets of journeymen
handed down in silence.
We the literate
one-time bowler-hatted
worked with letters
upside down and backwards
pressed onto pages
bound into books.

A closed-shop
the Father-of-the-Chapel
alert to any gripes.

Windowless walls
standing all day at the frame and stone
having a smoke in the earth-smelling 'bog'
missing out on an artists' revolution
introduced too young
to monotony.

Ragged Star

PART II

Ragged Star

I

Four a.m. along the canal
his boots splintering ice –
site of a dead man
overcoat, scarf and gloves on
soft hat rolled from his bald head –
hurrying, a butt flicked
sparking on the frozen water
at shifty rats
he made his way to the early shift
at Doran's bakery
feeding oven maws
stripped to the waist
bare feet on sacks
sweat dripping
until mid-day.

II

Four a.m. crossing the Liffey northwards
leaving hope
and protestant girls behind
seagulls squabbling
outside fast-food joints
along the grimy northside streets
family oriented and work
yards depots factories refineries
past tenements
the man with the jet black
butter-pasted hair watching
past an embedded huckster shop
Mrs Quigley offering small credit
between paroxysms of coughing
no trees little foliage
dusty privet maybe
further on
on terraced road and avenue
to bed to dream
of love not work
until mid-day.

III

He fumbled before me
came home at night
his key fumbling
at the hall door.
I went from home
at night
fumbling too
at heavy Georgian doors
opening on bulbless hallways
at bedsits and garden flats.

How do we explain ourselves
lives lived only half right?

IV

Head bowed
blowing on a burnt dinner
he couldn't rise
all gone
except her
and then her.
Haltingly
we skirted in her kitchen
picking up plates
where she left off.

V

He climbed the refinery's
dumb beasts at night
alone
circulation gone
hearing things
burned his feet
two blocks of ice
at the paraffin fire
fluid building
heart run down.

VI

From across the bay
I looked at his hump-backed city
the sun on the sea
like a shoal of fish
a lovers' rendezvous on the rocks
a wind-combed tree.
High on the winding path
a lunch-time cyclist
riding across the sea.

VII

I met her in a cafe booth
and kissed her on a stone seat
in a bedded
scent-colluding park
near a fountain.
I glimpsed a tuft
darker than her blonde hair
as we rose and fell
gasped and grasped
in the spray
on the cool grass esplanade.
Not really.
But her tongue did somersaults
in my mouth
at the band stand
before we parted
me for the six-weekly
barber's hand.

VIII

On a snowy December night
I walked a beauty home
to her garden flat.
Kiss greeted
she skirted in
praise-thanking
behind the jammy one
closing the door
citing the cold.

IX

I was sneaked in
bursting to go
out the window.
The stream alerted her.
Have you a man in your room, she asked?
No, she said.
Yes, I said, half naked.
I thought my torso
would save the day.
I walked home
under the disgusted trees
rain tut tutting
on the leaves.

X

It was never viable.
A brass bed in a tent
with the *King of the Travellers*
his pregnant wife 'Mouse' between us
patient, holding a candle flame
on her high stomach.
Father and son we had been earlier
around the camp fire
drinking something warm from a bottle
as sparks flew.
Dawning
I took my cue
and crawled away.

XI

Where did our libidos go?
His to horses, *True Detective*
fags and drink.

Mine to ruminating
Marxist, Existentialist, Nihilist
if only
where do I sign?
Shelter, surety.

Faithful to his wife.
Make your bed and lie in it.

I screwed at night
at day, vampire-like
slinked away
trawled through women
recalling her
calling to him?

XII

I believe in doubt
and worry disbelief.

After she died
I came upon him
in the garden shed
at prayer.
Embarrassed
struggling to his feet
he tried to cough it away.

XIII

His only stop
from pub to bed
was for a one an' one
in the FRIAR TUCK.
Amateur Angelo
Butlin's finalist *but the nerves*....
An Italian Dub
sang with verve
O Sole Mio
stirring chips
back to the appointed crowd.

XIV

I should have known
when a piece of twine –
gold braided in the sun
holding the gate shut
on an abandoned house –
was something I wished to look at
for an eternity.
But known what?

XV[4]

Advised to pack my DTs
for a drunken admission
pompous, but unnerved by
a dawn raid awakening.
Looking out the window
barred to keep me in
at those circling the grounds
looking to the sky
for something they had lost.
I walked back
across the highly polished sea
remembering
at my bed
a bowl of strawberries
shimmering.

[4] *The Irish poet Austin Clarke wrote a long poem entitled Mnemosyne Lay In Dust about his stay in St Patrick's Psychiatric Hospital. The above poem is a personal engagement with it.*

45

XVI

I err on the side of pessimism
alert to optimism
in case it might capsize me.
Reckless it can be
ludicrous, puny, unrealistic
unexamined.
Does my halting breath come from
buried grief?
Am I obdurate, obtuse
holding out against relief?
No, I have tried them all –
pendulums, sheep's enzymes
reiki, acupuncture, herbs
homeopathic pills
the most outlandish
just a memory in water.
All adding insult to injury.

Him? The chemist shop
on a Sunday
knock him up!
Dodo tablets for the chest
Andrew's Liver Salts the bowel.

XVII

Original fault line.
Engaged too early with death.
Freud's Oedipus trap.
Tap, tapping down to
Jung's collective.
Fate and fortune judgeless.
Grace.
Planets and stars
providing vindication.
Universal laws transgressed.
Stars fallen.
An albatross –
tell all *ad nausea*.

Marooned in the past.
All we can do –
Here son, pass me over those plates.

XVIII

I woke up flipped, dead?
Was somebody with me?
You should know in a single bed.
But with DTs
a donkey sits cross-legged
smoking a pipe and
unlike Pound's[5] petals on a bough
three faces look at me
evilly.

[5] *The American poet Ezra Pound*

IXX

Anseo, as láthair[6].
Absent fathers, lost sons.
Holding his finger in the flashing sun.
On his shoulders to see the match.
Is it that I couldn't get enough?
Aunty May said
That child's a craver.
And later on
another fearful fleeting visit
head around the door
oh, he's the image of him.

What was wrong with us?
Sins of his mother?
Sins of my father?
Ungenerous to say.
At his death bed
there'll never be another.

[6] *Present, absent as in school roll call.*

XX

I only want you to be happy.
Gulping against walloping
plaited tides
school and home respectively.
A truce
we'll cut the grass
don't forget that bit there.
I baulked at the verge
had enough, walked in
vertiginous.
You never finish anything.

XXI

It wasn't
The Man Who Killed Liberty Valance
with Jack Palance, no
regarding the family lore –
gruff, tough
tears leaked from him
in the sentimental darkness
of THE STRAND.
It might have been
The Greatest Story Ever Told?

XXII

He called my name
from a blind place.
Delirious one night
I'm going home
tried to
drips pulled from arms.
It seems it's common
with the dying.
Glad it wasn't only him.

XXIII

He left me alone
I told the cirrhosic night gotcha
stoking his stolen fire
on my way home.
Not at all!
He's watchin' over ye!
The house held memories
close to its chest
in spite of drink and drug venting.
Oh to be a Communist
to count the workers friends and all.
Subsiding into atavistic fears
somewhat righted by
the *Brandenburg Concertos*
and *The Ragged-Trousered Philanthropist.*

APOLOGIA

I could have done without
you dropping out
of the favour hard won
closed-shop printing trade
words not dough in hand
what you craved.
I could have done without
the bomb-shell hearse
to sell art from
get that thing out of here
with your nancy-boy friend.
I used to worry in the dark
did you bend?
I could have done without you railing
hammering madness
and us bereft
in the echo of the end
the last nail.

END